THE GREATEST
MOVIES
OF ALL TIME

HERRON & MURRAY

Exclusive Books, Gifts and Stationery

Est. 1980

First published in 2016
by Herron and Murray
www.herronandmurray.com

ISBN: 978-1-925449-08-1

Compiled by Lorri Lynn, Melody Bussey and Peter Murray

Images: Paramount Pictures, Columbia Pictures, Universal Pictures, United Artists, Selznick International Pictures, Metro-Goldwyn-Mayer, Warner Bros., RKO Radio Pictures, Orion Pictures, 20th Century Fox, DreamWorks Pictures (United States), Universal Pictures (International), Miramax Films, Embassy Pictures, Gramercy Pictures, Warner Bros.-Seven Arts, Focus Features

The author and publisher have made every effort to ensure the information contained in this book was correct at the time of going to press and accept no responsibility for any loss, injury or inconvenience sustained by any person or organisation using this book. Some editorial may have been used from the Public Domain.

Distributed world-wide by

CONTENTS

4 Introduction

8 The Godfather

10 The Shawshank Redemption

12 Schindler's List

14 Raging Bull

16 Casablanca

18 One Flew Over the Cuckoo's Nest

20 Gone with the Wind

22 Citizen Kane

24 The Wizard of Oz

26 Lawrence of Arabia

28 Sunset Boulevard

30 Psycho

32 The Godfather Part II

34 On the Waterfront

36 Vertigo

38 Forrest Gump

40 The Sound of Music

42 West Side Story

44 Star Wars

46 E.T. the Extra-Terrestrial

48 2001: A Space Odyssey

50 The Silence of the Lambs

52 Chinatown

54 The Bridge on the River Kwai

56 Singin' in the Rain

58 It's a Wonderful Life

60 Some Like It Hot

62 12 Angry Men

64 Dr. Strangelove

66 Amadeus

68 Ben-Hur

70 Apocalypse Now

72 The Lord of the Rings

74 Gladiator

76 From Here to Eternity

78 Titanic

80 Saving Private Ryan

82 Unforgiven

84 Raiders of the Lost Ark

86 Rocky

88 A Streetcar Named Desire

90 The Philadelphia Story

92 To Kill a Mockingbird

94 An American in Paris

96 The Best Years of Our Lives

98 My Fair Lady

100 A Clockwork Orange

102 Doctor Zhivago

104 Patton

106 Jaws

108 Braveheart

110 Butch Cassidy and the Sundance Kid

112 The Good, the Bad and the Ugly

114 The Treasure of the Sierra Madre

116 The Apartment

118 Platoon

120 High Noon

122 Dances with Wolves

124 The Pianist

126 Goodfellas

128 The Exorcist

130 The Deer Hunter

132 All Quiet on the Western Front

134 Bonnie and Clyde

136 The French Connection

138 City Lights

140 It Happened One Night

142 A Place in the Sun

144 Midnight Cowboy

146 Mr. Smith Goes to Washington

148 Rain Man

150 Annie Hall

152 Tootsie

154 Fargo

156 Giant

158 The Grapes of Wrath

160 Good Will Hunting

162 Shane

164 Terms of Endearment

166 The Green Mile

168 Close Encounters of the Third Kind

170 Network

172 The Graduate

174 American Graffiti

176 Pulp Fiction

178 The African Queen

180 Mutiny on the Bounty

182 The Maltese Falcon

Greatest Movies of All Time

Over the years, many have attempted to examine, label, and agree upon the greatest films in existence. While no one seems to agree completely on a single list, many of the movies, included on this list, were mentioned several times on several well-known lists, such as those generated by the film industry and reviewers. Most of the films mentioned herein are American films.

Since the late 1990s the American Film Institute regularly polled leaders for their top 100 choices for best film of a decade. Many of the perineal favourites came up time and time again, making those films obvious choices for

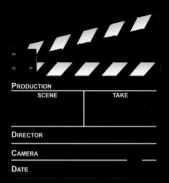

inclusion for a lifetime all best movie designation. What is evident, from an analysis of the current lists of 'best' nominees, all of the award winning movies have some similarities, such as they all revolve around a single conflict, that at first seems manageable, but then spirals out of control to include other oppositions that continue to enlarge until there are national, international, or intergalactic, ramifications. Through these conflicts and the dilemmas of the heroes, the truth of human living shines through, encouraging the viewer to believe in the struggle and the character.

upon a novel of the same name by Mario Puzo, who wrote the screenplay. Up until 1976 it held the record for being the highest grossing movie to date. It was directed by Francis Ford Coppola and featured Marlon Brando and Al Pacino. Together, they told the story of the Carleone family, a fictional mob operating out of New York during the 1940's and 1950's. What set the Godfather above other mafia movies is how the characters were portrayed. They weren't seen as one dimensional villains, but were instead richly nuanced and complex characters.

The Godfather™

upon the novella, Rita Hayworth and Shawsank Redemption, by Stephen King. The movie was written as well as directed by Frank Darabont. The movie starred Tim Robbins and Morgan Freeman. The story follows the imprisonment of two different inmates, and their quest to find solace and redemption in their new lives. The Shawshank Redemption failed at the box office when it was released in 1994. Despite failing in movie theaters, the film went on to be nominated for seven Oscars. This caused it to be re-released in the following year during Oscar season.

THE
SHAWSHANK
REDEMPTION
— 10TH ANNIVERSARY —

Oskar Schindler, who was a German businessman who saved the lives of many Jewish refugees during the Holocaust. Schindler's life story was first adapted into a novel by Thomas Keneally, titled Schindler's Ark. In 1993 Steven Spielberg adapted the novel into a film, starring Liam Neeson, Ralph Fiennes, and Ben Kingsley. The movie was shot for just a little over 22 million dollars, and ended up grossing over 320 million in box office sales. Critics worldwide praised the movie for its acting and cinematography.

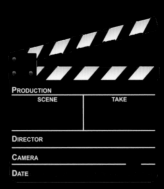

Raging Bull

Raging Bull is based on the memoirs of Jake LaMotta, titled Raging Bull: My Story. LaMotta was a famous Italian boxer with a very obsessive and destructive rage. His rage and jealousy ruined the relationship that he had with his wife and family. Martin Scorsese directed the film in 1980. The movie starred Robert De Niro, and two then unknown actors, Cathy Moriarty and Joe Pesci. The original reception to the film was quite mixed. Critics praised the performances, and Scorsese's choice to film in black and white garnered a great deal of praise.

Casablanca

Casablanca is based on an unproduced play, Everybody Comes to Rick's. It was turned into a romantic drama in 1942, directed by Michael Curtiz. The film included Humphrey Bogart, Ingrid Bergman, and Paul Henreid. The plot takes place in World War II and follows the story of an American who is forced to choose between his love for a woman and helping the Czech Resistance leader escape from the titular city of Casablanca so he can continue his fight against the Nazis. Superb acting and a host of memorable lines and a great soundtrack made it a timeless classic.

One Flew Over the Cuckoo's Nest

One Flew Over the Cuckoo's Nest, based on a novel by author Ken Kesey, was directed by Miloš Forman in 1975. The movie starred Jack Nicholson, Louise Fletcher, and Will Sampson. The movie follows the story of Randle Patrick McMurphy, is a prisoner who is sentenced to a mental institution after his arrest. The movie was an instant hit, and famously won the academy award for best picture, best actor, best actress, best director, and best screenplay. Only one film had previously done this.

Gone with the Wind

Gone with the Wind is based on a novel of the same name, written in 1936 by Margaret Mitchell. The story is centred around the South, during the American Civil War and the Reconstruction Era. The plot follows Scarlett O'Hara, the precocious daughter of a very rich and successful plantation owner. Scarlett is rendered poor after the war, and has to fight her way out of poverty. When accounting for inflation, it's still considered the highest grossing film in history. It was also famous for being the first movie where an African American won an Oscar.

DAVID O. SELZNICK'S PRODUCTION OF MARGARET MITCHELL'S

GONE WITH THE WIND

was produced, directed by, and starred Orson Welles. It was the first film that Welles ever wrote. It went on to get nominated for 9 different Academy Awards, even winning one for best writing. Since it was released, Citizen Kane has gone on to become one of the most famous movies ever to be produced. Even today, critics still praise the film, and it's considered to be the best movie of all time. The story follows the rise to fame of Charles Kane, a famous publisher.

The Wizard of Oz

The Wizard of Oz, based upon the book of the same name, was written in 1900 by L. Frank Baum. The film was directed in 1939 by Victor Flemming and starred Judy Garland, Ray Bolger, Jack Haley, Bert Lahr, Frank Morgan, Billie Burke, and Margaret Hamilton. The movie was famous for using Technicolor, as well as having such unique and fantastical characters. It was also acclaimed for having a strong musical score filled with original music. The film was the most expensive that had been produced at the time, costing a little over 2,750,000 dollars.

Lawrence of Arabia

Lawrence of Arabia is a 1962 historical drama film, directed by David Lean and based on the life of T.E. Lawrence. The film follows Lawrence's experiences in World War I, where he was in the Arabian Peninsula. The story largely focuses on Lawrence's involvement with the Arab National Council, as well as his attacks on Aqaba and Damascus. Critics praised the way that the film portrayed Lawrence's emotional struggles during the war, as he was forced to choose between his allegiance to his native home of Britain and the friends that he had made in the Arabian Peninsula.

LAWRENCE de ARABIA

[LAWRENCE OF ARABIA]

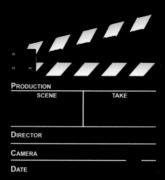

Sunset Boulevard

Sunset Boulevard is a 1950's black comedy and drama noir movie, both written and directed by Billy Wilder. The movie is named after the real boulevard that runs through Los Angeles and Beverly Hills. The film starred William Holden, Gloria Swanson, and Eric von Stroheim. The story follows a failed screenwriter, Joe Gillis, and a former silent movie star, Norma Desmond. Norma reaches out to Joe, pleading with him to writing a movie for her to star in so she can be famous again. Critics were fascinated with the dark views of Hollywood and fame, which hadn't been explored before.

SUNSET BOULEVARD

A HOLLYWOOD STORY

Psycho

Psycho was originally a novel, written in 1959 by Robert Bloch. The movie was written by Joseph Stefano, and famously directed by Alfred Hitchcock. The movie starred Anthony Perkins, Vera Miles, John Gavin, and Janet Leigh. The film follows Marion Crane, a secretary that steals money from her rich employer. While she's on the run she checks into a hotel, run by Norman Bates. Today, Psycho is considered to be Hitchcock's magnum opus. It was revolutionary at the time for having such an unexpected twist, as well as the unique way that violence was portrayed in the film.

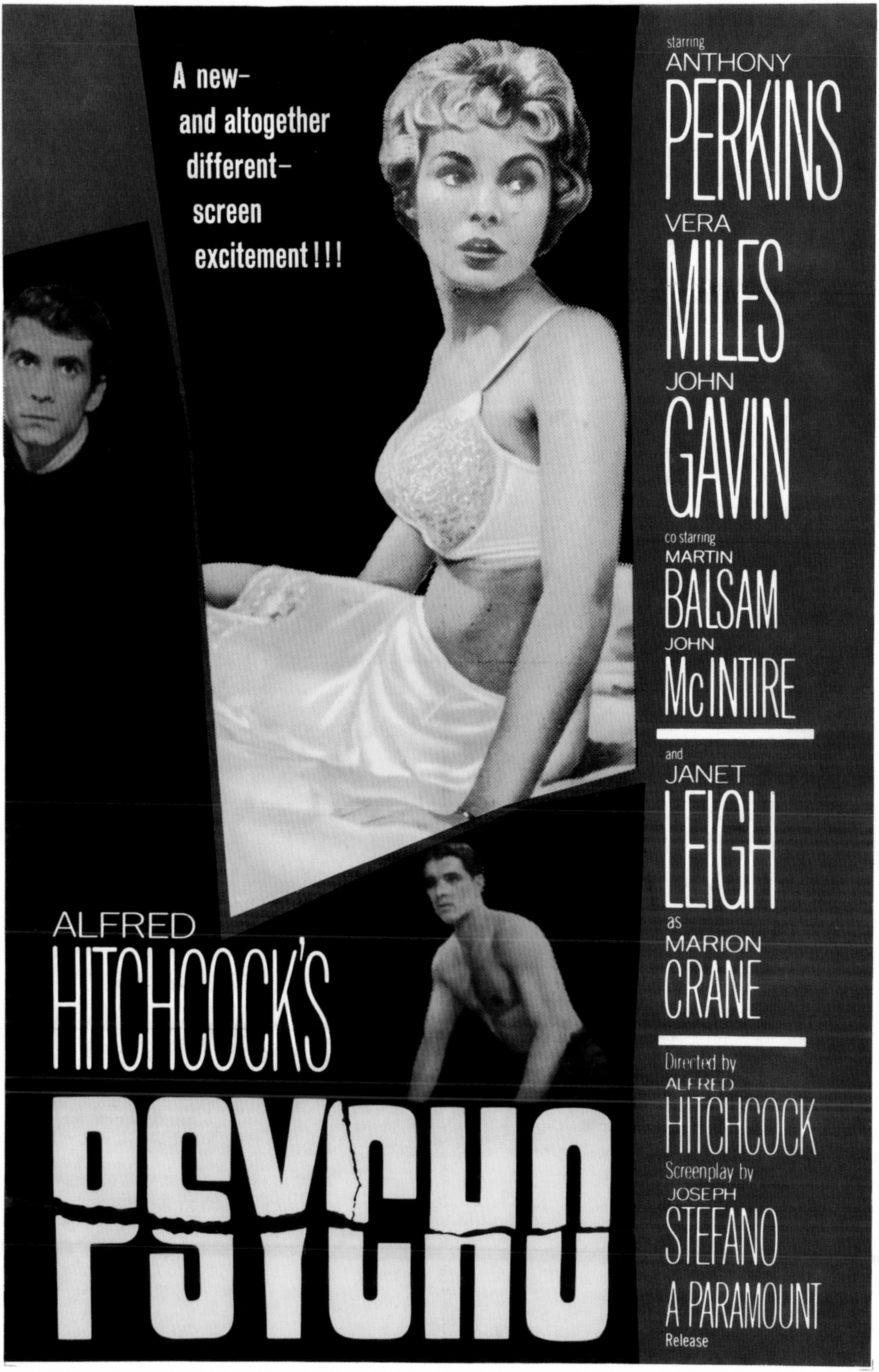
A new–
and altogether
different–
screen
excitement!!!
starring
ANTHONY
PERKINS
VERA
MILES
JOHN
GAVIN
co starring
MARTIN
BALSAM
JOHN
McINTIRE
and
JANET
LEIGH
as
MARION
CRANE
Directed by
ALFRED
HITCHCOCK
Screenplay by
JOSEPH
STEFANO
A PARAMOUNT
Release
ALFRED
HITCHCOCK'S
PSYCHO

The Godfather Part II

As the name suggests, the Godfather Part II is the sequel to the critically acclaimed Godfather. Both Al Pacino and Robert De Niro return to reprise their roles in the previous movie, and director Francis Ford Coppola was once again the director. The film is unique for being not only a sequel to the previous film, but also a prequel as well. It was the first sequel movie to ever win an Academy Award for best picture. As of 2015, no other film sequel boasts this claim.

drama with some elements of film noir, written by Budd Schulberg and directed by Elia Kazan. The movie is based on the stories, Crime on the Waterfront, which were published in the New York Sun by Malcolm Johnson in 1949. The movie starred Marlon Brando, Karl Maiden, Lee J. Cobb, Rob Steiger, and Eva Marie Saint. The story focuses on union violence for the longshoremen working in Hoboken, New Jersey. There were heavy plot elements featuring corruption, extortion, and racketeering in small town America.

PRODUCTION
SCENE   TAKE

DIRECTOR

CAMERA

DATE

Vertigo

Vertigo is another one of director Alfred Hitchcock's famous movies. Like his other hit movie, Psycho, Vertigo is based off of a novel, D'entre les morts, by author Boileau-Narcejac. This 1958 psychological thriller starred James Stewart and Kim Novak. The story follows a former police detective, John Ferguson. Ferguson is forced into early retirement because he developed a severe fear of heights, as well as suffering from a severe case of vertigo. Today, the movie is hailed for breaking many tropes that were common at the time, especially with its portrayal of such a flawed male protagonist.

JAMES STEWART
KIM NOVAK
IN ALFRED HITCHCOCKS
MASTERPIECE

'VERTIGO'

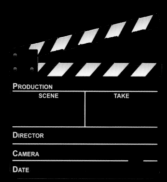

PRODUCTION
SCENE | TAKE

DIRECTOR

CAMERA

DATE

Forrest Gump

Forrest Gump, produced in 1994, is a romantic comedy/drama film. It was based off of a 1986 novel, written by Winston Groom. The movie was directed by Robert Zemeckis and starred Tom Hanks, Robin Wright, Gary Sinise, Sally Field, and Mykelti Williamson. The movie takes place over several decades, following the life of Forrest Gump. Gump is mentally very slow and naïve, but he has a good heart. The movie was well received for the way that it was able to blend its comedic elements while still having a very serious and dramatic story.

The Sound of Music

The Sound of Music is a 1965 musical film which was both produced and directed by Robert Wise. The movie is based upon a 1959 Broadway musical of the same name, originally composed by Richard Rodgers and Oscar Hammerstein II. The movie starred Julie Andrews and Christopher Plummer. The movie is about Maria, a free spirited young woman that's trying to become a nun in Salzburg, during 1938. Maria is sent to the home of a retired naval officer, acting as a governess for his 7 children. Critics praise the original score and the cinematography to help tell the story.

20th CENTURY FOX *presents*

RODGERS *and* HAMMERSTEIN'S

A ROBERT WISE *Production*

THE SOUND OF MUSIC

Produced in TODD-AO
COLOR BY DE LUXE

Starring JULIE **ANDREWS** · CHRISTOPHER **PLUMMER**

Co-starring **RICHARD HAYDN** *With* PEGGY WOOD, CHARMIAN CARR, THE BIL BAIRD MARIONETTES *And* **ELEANOR PARKER** *as The Baroness*

Associate Producer SAUL CHAPLIN

Directed by **ROBERT WISE** | *Music by* **RICHARD RODGERS** | *Lyrics by* **OSCAR HAMMERSTEIN II**

Additional Words and Music by Richard Rodgers

Screenplay by **ERNEST LEHMAN** | *Production Designed by* BORIS LEVEN
Produced by Argyle Enterprises, Inc.

West Side Story

West Side Story is the film adaptation of a 1957 musical Broadway of the same name. The original composers were Leonard Bernstein, and Stephen Sondheim. The film version came out in 1961 and was directed by Robert Wise and Jerome Robbins. The movie starred Natalie Woods, Richard Beymer, Russ Tamblyn, Rita Moreno, and George Chakiris. The story follows two rival gangs, the Sharks and the Jets. Two of the gang members, Tony and Maria, fall in love with one another, despite being on opposing sides. It's considered to be one of the most iconic adaptations of Romeo and Juliet.

Unlike other classics "West Side Story" grows younger!

"BEST PICTURE!" Winner of 10 Academy Awards! — 1961

WEST SIDE STORY

MIRISCH PICTURES PRESENTS "WEST SIDE STORY" A ROBERT WISE PRODUCTION

STARRING NATALIE WOOD

RICHARD BEYMER · RUSS TAMBLYN · RITA MORENO · GEORGE CHAKIRIS DIRECTED BY ROBERT WISE AND JEROME ROBBINS
SCREENPLAY BY ERNEST LEHMAN ASSOCIATE PRODUCER SAUL CHAPLIN · CHOREOGRAPHY BY JEROME ROBBINS MUSIC BY LEONARD BERNSTEIN LYRICS BY STEPHEN SONDHEIM
BASED UPON THE STAGE PLAY PRODUCED BY ROBERT E. GRIFFITH AND HAROLD S. PRINCE · BOOK BY ARTHUR LAURENTS PLAY CONCEIVED, DIRECTED AND CHOREOGRAPHED BY JEROME ROBBINS
FILM PRODUCTION DESIGNED BY BORIS LEVEN · MUSIC CONDUCTED BY JOHNNY GREEN · FILMED IN PANAVISION® · TECHNICOLOR® PRESENTED BY MIRISCH PICTURES, INC. IN ASSOCIATION WITH SEVEN ARTS PRODUCTIONS, INC.

Star Wars

Star Wars is a space opera that was filmed in 1977, and was written and directed by George Lucas. The film starred Mark Hamill, Harrison Ford, Carrie Fisher, Peter Cushing, and Alec Guinness. It was later retitled to Star Wars Episode IV: A New Hope after the critical success of the movie. The story takes place in another galaxy and follows the attempts of Princess Leia and the rebel Alliance to overthrow the tyrannical Galactic Empire. Star Wars was praised for its special effects, and has been credited as breathing life back into the science fiction drama.

TWENTIETH CENTURY-FOX Presents A LUCASFILM LTD. PRODUCTION STAR WARS
Starring MARK HAMILL HARRISON FORD CARRIE FISHER
PETER CUSHING
and
ALEC GUINNESS

Written and Directed by   Produced by   Music by
GEORGE LUCAS   GARY KURTZ   JOHN WILLIAMS
PANAVISION® PRINTS BY DE LUXE® TECHNICOLOR®

Making Films Sound Better
DOLBY SYSTEM®
Noise Reduction · High Fidelity

Original Motion Picture Soundtrack on 20th Century Records and Tapes

© 1977 20TH CENTURY-FOX

PRINTED IN U.S.A.   ONE SHEET STYLE "C"

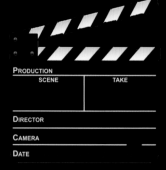

E.T. the Extra-Terrestrial

E.T. is a 1982 science fiction movie, directed by Steven Spielberg and written by Melissa Mathison. It starred Henry Thomas, Dee Wallace, Robert MacNaughton, Drew Barrymore, and Peter Coyote. The story is centred around a young boy, Elliott, who is lonely. He ends up discovering an extraterrestrial, which he nicknames as E.T. E.T. was a huge hit, famously beating out Star Wars as the highest grossing film of all time. Even today, film critics praise the movie for the way that it portrays friendship between the characters.

A STEVEN SPIELBERG FILM

E.T.

THE EXTRA-TERRESTRIAL
IN HIS ADVENTURE ON EARTH

that was directed, produced, and co-written by Stanley Kubrick, along with Arthur C. Clarke. The movie starred Keir Dullea and Gary Lockwood. The story follows an astronaut, Dr. David Bowman, sent to the planet Jupiter after the discovery of a mysterious monolith, which is believed to have an effect on humanity's evolution. Bowman is accompanied on his journey by the sentient computer, HAL. What made 2001 so unique was the way that it was shot. The movie uses a sparse amount of dialogue, relying largely on musical cues to help tell the story.

2001: a space odyssey

MGM PRESENTS A STANLEY KUBRICK PRODUCTION

CINERAMA® Super Panavision®
and Metrocolor

PRODUCTION
SCENE   TAKE

DIRECTOR

CAMERA

DATE

The Silence of the Lambs

Silence of the Lambs was originally a novel, written in 1988 by Thomas Harris. It was adapted into a movie in 1991, directed by Jonathan Demme. It starred Jodie Foster, Anthony Hopkins, and Scott Glenn. The film is about a young FBI trainee, Clarice Starling, who is trying to catch a serial killer, Buffalo Bill. Clarice has to work with Dr. Hannibal Lecter. Lecter was imprisoned for being a serial killer who ate his victims. The movie is famous for introducing the world to the character of Hannibal Lecter. Audiences found him to be a fascinating and genuinely terrifying character.

the silence of the lambs

a major motion picture

Chinatown

There have been a few different movies that have been titled Chinatown, but the most famous is the mystery/film noir film written by Robert Towne and directed by Roman Polanski in 1974. The movie was loosely inspired by the California Water Wars, which were disputes about water in the southern parts of California. Critics loved the film because it brought so much public awareness to land dealings and disputes over water rights. Chinatown is also hailed as being the movie that launched Jack Nicholson's acting career.

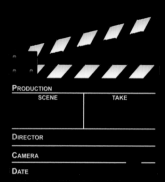

PRODUCTION

SCENE | TAKE

DIRECTOR

CAMERA

DATE

The Bridge on the River Kwai

The Bridge on the River Kwai was originally a novel released in 1952 by Pierre Boulle. The film was released in 1957, directed by David Lean. It starred William Holden, Jack Hawkins, Alec Guinness, and Sessue Hayakawa. The story takes place in World War II. A group of British prisoners arrive in a Japanese prison camp where they are sentenced to work on building a railway bridge over the River Kwai, which would connect Bangkok and Rangoon. While the movie features fictional events, they're based upon conditions that prisoners really underwent when constructing the Burma Railway.

Singin' in the Rain

Singin' in the Rain is a 1952 musical comedy directed by Gene Kelly and Stanley Donen. It starred Gene Kelly, Donald O'Connor and Debbie Reynolds. The movie takes place in Hollywood during the late 1920's. It was right around this time where movies were transitioning from being silent films into talkies. The story follows the production of a two silent movie stars, Don Lockwood and Lina Lamont. Singin' in the Rain was praised for telling a serious story without losing the light hearted comedic tones, as well as the impressive shots and songs all throughout the movie.

It's a Wonderful Life

It's a Wonderful Life is a 1946 fantasy/drama set during Christmas. The movie was directed and produced by Frank Capra, but the movie itself is actually based on a 1939 short story by Philip Van Doren Stern. It starred James Stewart and Henry Travers. The plot follows the character of George Bailey, who has given up on his life and decides that he is going kill himself on Christmas Eve. He is contacted by an angel, Clarence Odbody, who shows him what life would be like without him. The film ended up becoming a classic when it was released in the late 1970's on Christmas.

Some Like It Hot

This 1959 film was directed and produced by Billy Wilder. It starred the famous actress Marilyn Monroe, Tony Curtis, and Jack Lemmon. The story is about two musicians that witness the mafia committing the Saint Valentine's Day Massacre. The two musicians have to disguise themselves as being part of an all-female band in order to escape. It was shot in black and white because there were too many colour limitations to make the main characters appear authentic with their costumes. This helped the film because it was set in the 20's, so the black and white gave it an authentic feel.

12 Angry Men

The 1957 version of 12 Angry Men is based upon a teleplay with the same name, written by Reginald Rose. The movie version was written and co-produced by Rose, but directed by Sidney Lumet. The story takes place in New York City. Twelve jurors are deciding the fate of an 18 year old from the slums, who's on trial for supposedly stabbing his father to death. 11 of the 12 jurors almost instantly agree on finding him guilty, but Juror 8 votes not guilty. One theme the critics loved was how quick some people are to judge someone based on their prejudices.

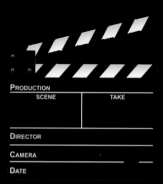

Dr. Strangelove

Dr. Strangelove is a 1964 political satire/black comedy, directed, produced and co-written by Stanley Kubrick. It starred Peter Sellers, George C. Scott, Sterling Hayden, Keenan Wynn, and Slim Pickens. The story follows a few different characters. It starts off with a disgruntled Air Force general ordering a nuclear strike against the Soviet Union. The story then follows the President of the United States and his advisors, the Joint Chiefs of Staff, as well as the Royal Air Force all trying to bring the bombers home. Dr. Strangelove is still considered to be one of the best political satires of all time.

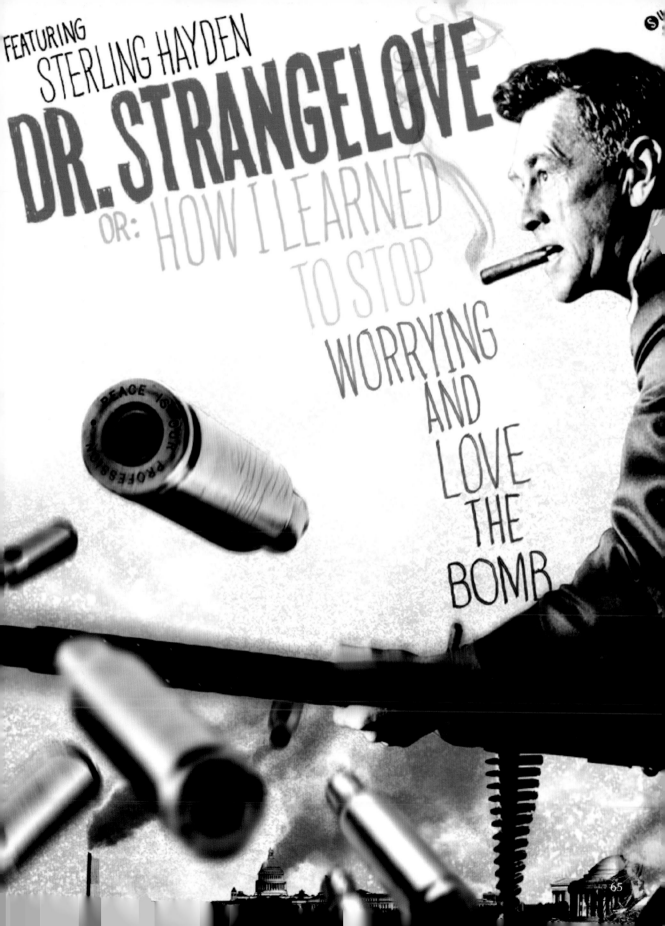

FEATURING STERLING HAYDEN

DR. STRANGELOVE

OR: HOW I LEARNED TO STOP WORRYING AND LOVE THE BOMB

Amadeus

Amadeus is a 1984 period drama, written by Peter Shaffer and directed by Miloš Forman. The movie is actually an adaptation of Shaffer's stage play by the same name. The movie stars F. Murray Abraham, Tom Hulce, Elizabeth Berridge, Simon Callow, Roy Dotrice, Christine Ebersole, Jeffrey Jones, and Charles Kay. The movie opens in 1823, with Antonio Salieri attempting suicide, screaming for forgiveness for killing Wolfgang Amadeus Mozart. Amadeus was a huge hit at the box offices. In 1985, it was nominated for eleven Academy Awards.

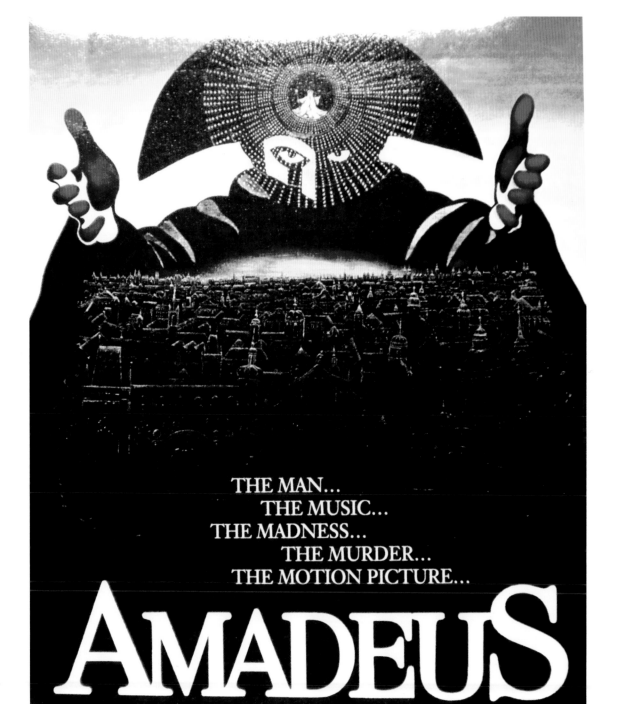

THE MAN...
THE MUSIC...
THE MADNESS...
THE MURDER...
THE MOTION PICTURE...

AMADEUS

Ben-Hur

There have been multiple moves about Ben-Hur, but the most famous is the 1959 epic directed by William Wyler, and starring Charlton Heston, Stephen Boyd, Jack Hawkins, Hugh Griffith, and Haya Harareet. The story follows the titular character, Judah Ben-Hur, a wealthy prince and merchant from Jerusalem who is enslaved for his beliefs. At the time, Ben-Hur had the largest budget of any movement, a little over 15 million. It also boasted having the largest sets built for any film produced at the time. As of 2015, it is the second highest grossing film in history.

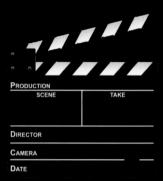

Apocalypse Now

Apocalypse Now is a 1979 film that is based on the novel, Heart of Darkness, by Joseph Conrad. The screenplay was written by John Milus, and the director, Francis Ford Coppola. The movie starred Martin Sheen, Marlon Brando, and Robert Duvall. The story is about Captain Benjamin Willard being sent on a secret mission to assassinate Colonel Walter Kurtz, a soldier with the Special Forces who had gone insane and commands his own private army inside of Cambodia. The film was praised for the dark portrayal of the Vietnam War. While the film was a huge success, it's also become famous for behind the scenes trouble.

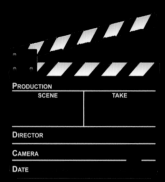

The Lord of the Rings: The Return of the King

The Return of the King is the final part of the Lord of the Rings trilogy, based on the famous fantasy book series of the same name, written by J.R.R. Tolkien in 1954. The movie follows the story of the Hobbit, Frodo Baggins, on the final leg of his journey to destroy the Ring, a magical artifact that the Dark Lord Sauron is after in order to rule all of Middle Earth. As of 2015, it is the 12th highest grossing film in history. It also famously won all of the 11 Academy Awards that it was nominated for.

THE LORD OF THE RINGS
THE RETURN OF THE KING ™
(LE SEIGNEUR DES ANNEAUX : LE RETOUR DU ROI)
WINNER OF 11 ACADEMY AWARDS®
INCLUDING BEST PICTURE 2003
©A.M.P.A.S.®
DVD
ALLIANCE ATLANTIS

Gladiator

There have been several films over the years with the name of Gladiator. It's the 2000 version of Gladiator, directed by Ridley Scott, which is the most famous. The movie starred Russell Crowe, Joaquin Phoenix, Connie Nielson, Ralf Möller, Djimon Hounsou, Derek Jacobi, John Sharpnel, Richard Harris, and in his final role, Oliver Reed. The movie is about Roman general, Maximus Decimus Meridius. He's betrayed by the son of the Emperor, Commodus, who also killed his father to rise to power. Gladiator has been credited as restoring interest to the historical epic genre.

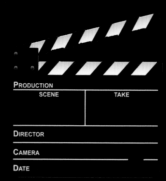

From Here to Eternity

From Here to Eternity produced in 1953 was directed by Fred Zinnemann. It was based on a novel written by James Jones. The film starred Burt Lancaster, Montgomery Clift, Frank Sinatra, Deborah Kerr, and Donna Reed. The movie follows the lives of three soldiers serving in Hawaii, months before the attack on Pearl Harbor. The film went on to get great reviews from the critics. The acting in particular was praised, with many being taken away by the strong performance from Frank Sinatra. Critics enjoyed how true to life the drama was.

produced, co-edited, and directed by James Cameron. The movie starred Leonardo DiCaprio and Kate Winslet. The movie is a fictionalized account of the famous sinking of the RMS Titanic in 1912. The film follows the story of Rose DeWitt Bukater and Jack Dawson. Rose is a first class passenger on the titanic, along with her mother and her fiancé, Cal Hockley. Rose is being forced into the marriage because it will save her family from financial ruin. Titanic was instantly a huge hit, getting nominated for 14 Academy awards. Titanic was the first film to ever gross more than 1 billion dollars.

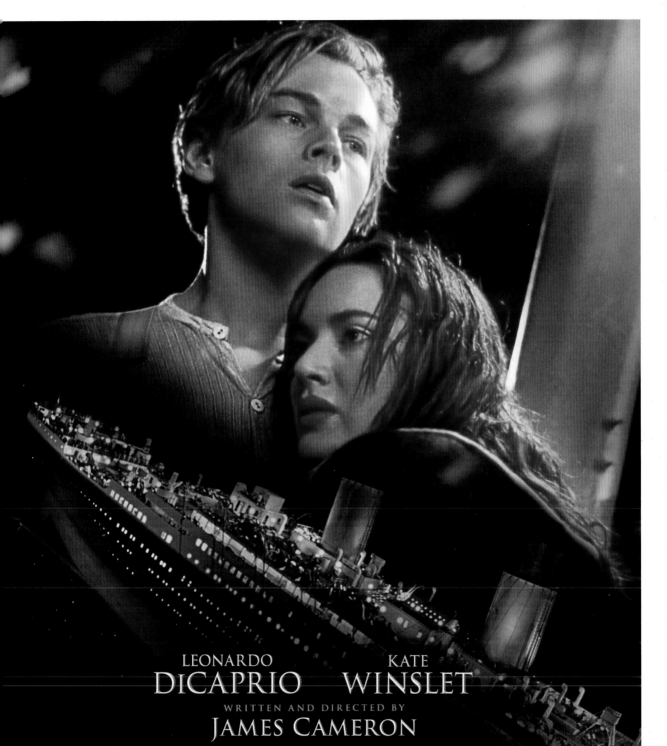

LEONARDO   KATE
DICAPRIO   WINSLET
WRITTEN AND DIRECTED BY
JAMES CAMERON

TITANIC

Saving Private Ryan

Saving Private Ryan is a war drama that was directed by Steven Spielberg and written by Robert Rodat in 1998. The film takes place in World War II, during the invasion of Normandy. Three of the four Ryan brothers are killed during the battle. The last, James Francis Ryan, was reported as missing in action. General George Marshall is tasked with finding Ryan and bringing him home. One of the scenes that the movie was most famous for was the Omaha Beach landing. Even today, this is considered to be one of the best battle sequences of all time.

A STEVEN SPIELBERG FILM

tom hanks

saving private ryan

edward burns   matt damon   tom sizemore

the mission is a man.

DREAMWORKS PICTURES AND PARAMOUNT PICTURES PRESENT
AN AMBLIN ENTERTAINMENT PRODUCTION IN ASSOCIATION WITH MUTUAL FILM COMPANY TOM HANKS "SAVING PRIVATE RYAN"
EDWARD BURNS MATT DAMON TOM SIZEMORE CO-PRODUCERS BONNIE CURTIS AND ALLISON LYON SEGAN MUSIC BY JOHN WILLIAMS
COSTUME DESIGNER JOANNA JOHNSTON FILM EDITOR MICHAEL KAHN, A.C.E. PRODUCTION DESIGNER TOM SANDERS DIRECTOR OF PHOTOGRAPHY JANUSZ KAMINSKI, A.S.C.
PRODUCED BY STEVEN SPIELBERG & IAN BRYCE AND MARK GORDON & GARY LEVINSOHN WRITTEN BY ROBERT RODAT
DIRECTED BY STEVEN SPIELBERG

RESTRICTED R
UNDER 17 REQUIRES ACCOMPANYING
PARENT OR ADULT GUARDIAN

DOLBY DIGITAL

SDDS Sony Dynamic Digital Sound

dts DIGITAL SOUND

AMBLIN

SOUNDTRACK AVAILABLE ON

DREAMWORKS PICTURES

81

was directed, produced, and starred Clint Eastwood. Eastwood starred alongside Gene Hackman, Morgan Freeman, and Richard Harris. It was the last western project that Eastwood wanted to do. Eastwood wanted to make a darker western that dealt with violence and the complicated truths behind many of the old western stories. The story starts with Delilah Fitzgerald who is being disfigured by two cowboys, Quick Mike and Davey-Boy Bunting. The sheriff simply makes them pay a fine to the brothel where she worked. The other prostitutes are upset with this and place a bounty on the two cowboys.

THE UNFORGIVEN

Raiders of the Lost Ark

Raiders of the Lost Ark is the first official Indiana Jones movie. It was directed by Steven Spielberg, with the screenplay being written by Lawrence Kasdan, Philip Kaufman, and George Lucas. The movie starred Harrison Ford, Karen Allen, Paul Freeman, Ronald Lacey, John Rhys-Davies, and Denholm Elliott. The story follows an archaeologist named Indiana Jones. Jones is recruited by the Army to help them find the legendary Ark of the Covenant. When adjusted for inflation, Raiders of the Lost Ark ranks amongst the top twenty highest grossing films of all time, and it helped to popularize the action adventure genre.

that was directed by John G. Avildsen. It was written by and featured Sylvester Stallone in the lead role. Talia Shire, Burt Young, Carl Weathers, and Burgess Meredith also starred alongside Stallone. The movie is about the titular character, Rocky Balboa. Rocky is an uneducated, but overall a very kind hearted Italian-American boxer. Rocky ends up getting a once in a lifetime opportunity to go into the boxing ring with the world heavyweight champion, Apollo Creed. Critics appreciated that Rocky was willing to tell a rags to riches story, something that had been cast aside in favour of darker and more melodramatic plots.

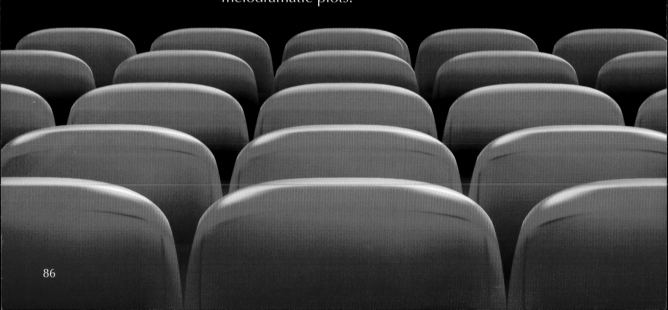

A Streetcar Named Desire

A Streetcar Named Desire is based on the 1947 play by Tennessee Williams. The story follows Blanche DuBois, a high school teacher that decides to leave her home in Mississippi, travel to New Orleans so she can live with her sister, Stella. Stella is married to Stanley Kowalski. They live in a very small, run down two room apartment. Blanche is surprised, especially when she learns that Stanley is an abusive husband who clearly has no respect for Stella. The movie was instantly praised for exploring such dark themes. Streetcar was the first film to win three different Oscar's for acting categories.

The Philadelphia Story

The Philadelphia Story is a 1940 romantic comedy, based upon a Broadway play of the same name, which was written by Phillip Barry. The film was directed by George Cukor, and starred Cary Grant, Katharine Hepburn, James Stewart, and Ruth Hussey. The story follows Tracy Lord, a wealthy socialite in Philadelphia. She recently divorced her husband, C. K. Dexter Haven. She's getting ready to marry George Kittredge, which is believed to be the wedding of the century. In 1940 The Philadelphia Story had set the bar high for comedic writing. Film critics raved about how well the actors played off of one another.

Cary GRANT

James STEWART

Katharine HEPBURN

The Philadelphia Story

To Kill a Mockingbird

To Kill a Mockingbird is a 1962 dramatic film, based off of the book of the same name written by Harper Lee. The movie was directed by Robert Mulligan and written by Horton Foote. It starred Gregory Peck, Mary Badham, Philip Alford, John Megna, Ruth White, Paul Fix, Brock Peters, and Frank Overton. The story takes place in the 1930's, following two children, Jean Louise Finch and Jeremy Atticus Finch. Their father, Atticus, is a lawyer representing a black man, Tom Robinson, who is being accused of raping a young white woman. Film critics praise Gregory Peck's performance as Atticus Finch.

An American in Paris

An American in Paris was originally a 1928 orchestral composition, created by George Gershwin, and adapted into a 1951 musical by Vincente Minnelli. The movie starred Gene Kelly, Leslie Caron, Oscar Levant, Nina Foch, and Georges Guétary. All of the music was written by George Gershwin and his brother, Ira. The plot follows A World War II veteran, Jerry Mulligan, who is trying to make a career for himself as an artist in Paris. Part of what made An American in Paris such a famous movie was the climatic dance, which was a 16 minute long ballet.

The Best Years of Our Lives

The Best Years of Our Lives is a 1946 drama, directed by William Wyler. The film starred Myrna Loy, Fredric March, Dana Andrews, Teresa Wright, Virginia Mayo, and Harold Russell. The story follows the lives of three soldiers returning home from World War II, Fred Derry, Homer Parrish, and Al Stephenson. Each soldier faces a different difficulty returning home. The Best Years of Our Lives went on to be the highest grossing film since the release of Gone with the Wind.

RNA LOY   FREDRIC MARCH   DANA ANDREWS   TERESA WRIGHT

SAMUEL GOLDWYN PRESENTS

The Best Years of Our Lives

WINNER OF
8 ACADEMY AWARDS
INCLUDING
BEST PICTURE
(1946)

©A.M.P.A.S.®

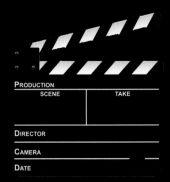

My Fair Lady

My Fair Lady is a 1964 musical. It starred Audrey Hepburn, Rex Harrison, Stanley Holloway, Wilfrid Hyde-White, Gladys Cooper, and Jeremy Brett. The story takes place in London at the turn of the century. Professor Henry Higgins is a scholar of phonetics. He's famous for believing that someone's voice and the way they speak ultimately determines where they end up in society. He makes a wager with one of his acquaintances, Hugh Pickering, that he could pick any person at random and pass them off as being a duke or duchess.

AUDREY
HEPBURN

REX
HARRISON

MY FAIR LADY

A Clockwork Orange

A Clockwork Orange was a 1971 crime film which was directed, produced, and written by Stanley Kubrick. The film was based on a 1962 novel of the same name, which was written by Anthony Burgess. It follows the story of a violent criminal, Alex DeLarge. His gang betrays him and Alex is arrested. While in prison, the Minister of the Interior picks him to be a test subject for something called the Ludovico technique, a type of aversion therapy that can supposedly cure a criminal of their violent behaviour. The film was very controversial for its portrayal of violence.

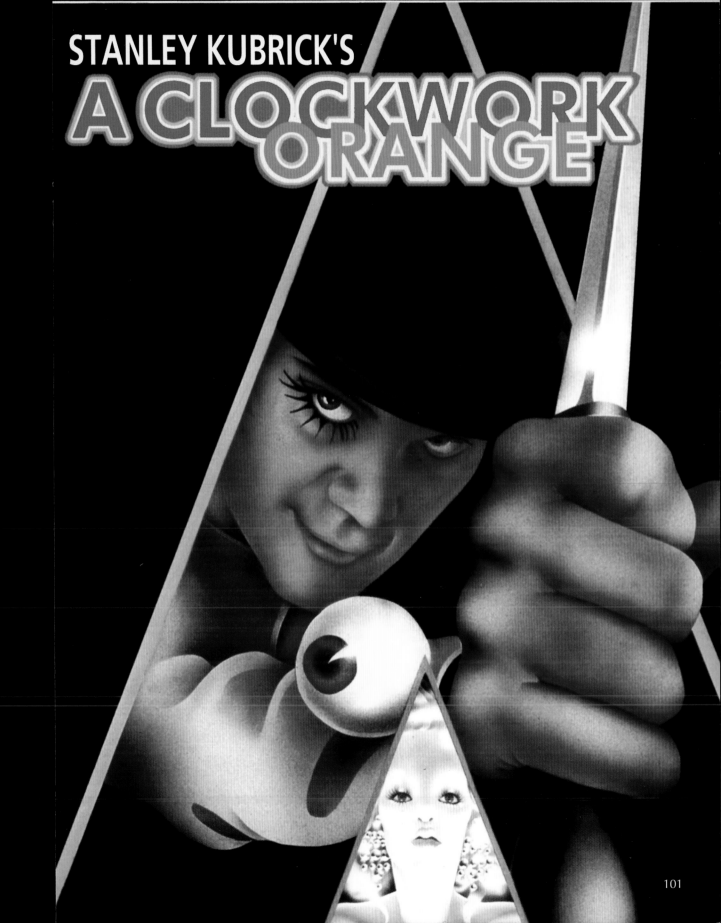

Doctor Zhivago

Doctor Zhivago was first a novel, written in 1957 by author Boris Pasternak. The movie was released in 1965, directed by David Lean and written by Robert Bolt. It starred Omar Sharif, Alec Guinness, and Julie Christie. The movie takes place primarily in Russian, right before World War I. It follows the life of Yefgraf Andreyevich Zhivago as he searches for his half-brother, Doctor Yuri Andreyevich Zhivago. He discovers a young woman who he believes to be his niece. He tells her about the life of her father, the enigmatic Doctor Zhivago, and his life during the Russian Revolution.

DOCTOR ZHIVAGO

Patton

Patton is a war film that tells the story of General George S. Patton during World War II. The 1970 movie was based on two different books, Patton: Ordeal and Triumph by Ladislas Farago, and A Soldier's Story by Omar Bradley. Bradley also served as a military consultant throughout the whole film. The movie was directed by Franklin J. Schaffner and starred George C. Scott, Karl Malden, Michael Bates, and Karl Michael Vogler. George C. Scott was praised for his role as Patton, with many film critics citing the success of the movie was from Scott's undeniably strong performance.

Jaws

Jaws is a 1975 horror/thriller movie directed by Steven Spielberg. The movie was based on the novel by Peter Benchley, bearing the same name. The film takes place on Amity Island, at the start of tourist season. There's a shark attack, and the chief of police, Brody, argues with the Mayor that they need to shut down the beaches. Jaws was an instant cinematic hit, becoming the highest grossing film of all time, a title that it held until the release of Star Wars. John Williams was praised for the musical composition that was developed to help support the story.

Braveheart

Braveheart is a 1995 historical war drama, directed by and starring Mel Gibson. Braveheart follows the story of William Wallace, a Scottish farmer that gets pulled into the war with his oppressive English rulers after they start murdering his countrymen, including his wife. Braveheart is loosely based on historical events, namely old legends that were passed down in poems. Braveheart was not only a commercial success, but it also helped to increase tourism in Scotland. It also increased the overall interest in Scottish history.

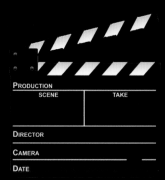

Butch Cassidy and the Sundance Kid

Butch Cassidy and the Sundance Kid is a film, directed by George Roy Hill. It starred Paul Newman, Robert Redford, Katherine Ross, Strother Martin, Jeff Corey, and Henry Jones. The 1969 story is inspired by real events, telling the life and times of western outlaws Robert LeRoy Parker and Harry Longabaugh, better known as Butch Cassidy and Sundance Kid. In 2013, the Writers Guild of America ranked Butch Cassidy and the Sundance Kid as number 11 on their list of 101 greatest screenplays of all time. Overall, it ranks as the 34th highest grossing film of all time.

PAUL NEWMAN   ROBERT REDFORD

BUTCH CASSIDY
AND THE SUNDANCE KID

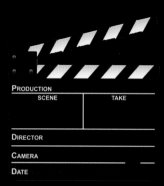

The Good, the Bad and the Ugly

The Good, the Bad, and the Ugly is a film that was shot as a Spaghetti Western Film in 1966. It was directed by Sergio Leone and starred Clint Eastwood, Lee Van Cleef, and Eli Wallach. The story follows three different bandits, Tuco, Angel Eyes, and Blondie, all of which are trying to get the same stash of hidden Confederate gold. The Good, the Bad and the Ugly is seen as being one of the quintessential western movies. Leone was praised for his use of stylistic gunfights, as well as his choices in using a mixture of long and close shots to help create dramatic tension.

The Treasure of the Sierra Madre

The Treasure of the Sierra Madre, made in 1948, is an adventure/western drama, with some elements of film noir. It was directed and written by John Huston, who based it off of a 1927 novel of the same name. The story follows Fred Dobbs and Bob Curtin, who are two Americans who have come to Mexico to find work. They convince a prospector to show them how to dig in the Sierra Madre Mountains for gold. This was the first time that an American movie was filmed outside of the United States. It was among the first 100 films preserved by the National Film Registry.

The Apartment

The Apartment is a comedy/drama that was written, produced, and directed by Billy Wilder in 1960. It starred Jack Lemmon, Shirley MacLaine, and Fred MacMurray. The story follows Calvin Clifford, a poor office worker who tries to raise his standings by loaning out his apartment to his bosses to use for their affairs. The film was very controversial at the time for being a comedy about adultery and infidelity. Despite that, it was a huge hit and was nominated for 10 Academy Awards, even winning best picture for that year.

Platoon

Platoon is a war film, both written and directed by Oliver Stone in 1986. The movie starred Tom Berenger, Willem Dafoe, and Charlie Sheen. The story takes place during Vietnam. Chris Taylor, a college dropout, enlists in the army. He's assigned to the 25th infantry division fighting at the Cambodian border. Film critics praised Oliver Stone's depiction of the Vietnam War, capturing the darkness of the war without coming off as being preachy. The movie was partially inspired by Stone's real life experiences in Vietnam.

An OLIVER STONE Film

PLATOON

The first

casualty

of war is

innocence.

ACADEMY AWARD®
WINNER
"BEST PICTURE"
1986
©AMPAS®

written by Carl Foreman and directed by Fred Zinnemann. It starred Gary Cooper, Grace Kelly, and Ian MacDonald. The story follows Will Kane, a marshal in the New Mexico Territory. He just got married and decided to retire, but a criminal that Kane had previously arrested is about to head into town, having gotten off on a legal technicality. High Noon was famous for deconstructing the western drama. It didn't feature the usual elements of a western, but instead focused on heavy dialogue and the emotional and moral instincts of the characters.

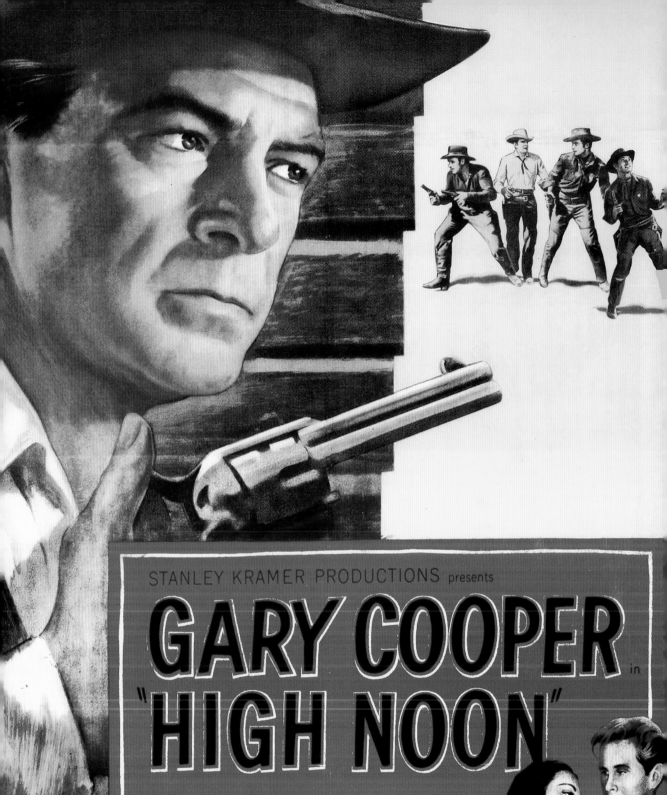

STANLEY KRAMER PRODUCTIONS presents

GARY COOPER in

"HIGH NOON"

Dances with Wolves

Dances with Wolves is a 1990 western film, produced, directed and starring Kevin Costner. The movie is an adaptation of a 1988 book by Michael Blake, also titled Dancing with Wolves. It also starred Mary McDonnel, Graham Greene, and Rodney A. Grant. The story follows Lt. John Dunbar, who is sent to a remote outpost during the Civil War. While there, he befriends a wolf, and later the native people living there, making him an aberration to the rest of the military. The film was a surprise hit of the year, with critics quite impressed with the way that the Native American's were portrayed.

KEVIN COSTNER

DANCES WITH WOLVES

The Pianist

The Pianist is a 2002 historical drama, directed by Roman Polanski. The story is based on an autobiography, The Pianist, by composer Wladyslaw Szpilman. The movie follows Szpilman's life through the German invasion of Poland during World War II. The Pianist is hailed as Polanski's best work. Polanski himself felt a powerful connection with the story, since he had just managed to escape from the Kraków Ghetto when he was a child. Critics were surprised with the strong performance by Adrien Brody, who won several awards for his portrayal of Szpilman.

A ROMAN POLANSKI FILM

THE PIANIST

MUSIC WAS HIS PASSION. SURVIVAL WAS HIS MASTERPIECE.

Goodfellas is based on the 1986 non-fiction book written by Nicholas Pileggi. Pileggi worked on the screenplay with director Martin Scorsese. The movie starred Robert De Niro, ray Liotta, Joe Pesci, Lorraine Bracco, and Paul Sorvino. The story follows Henry Hill, who quits school and decides to climb up the ranks of a mafia family. All of the actors were praised for their performances. Scorsese was credited with making every shot count and last just as long as it needed to. Some critics were even calling it a modern day version of the Godfather when it first premiered.

ROBERT DE NIRO

AY LIOTTA

JOE PESCI

"As far back as I can remember, I've always wanted
to be a gangster."
–Henry Hill, Brooklyn, N.Y. 1955.

GoodFellas

A MARTIN SCORSESE PICTURE

Three Decades of Life in the Mafia.

The Exorcist

The Exorcist is a 1973 horror film directed by William Friedkin. It was adapted from a book of the same name, written by William Peter Blatty in 1971. It starred Linda Blair, Ellen Burstyn, Jason Miller, and Max Von Sydow. The story follows the possession of a young child, Regan, by a demon, and the attempts of two priests to exorcise the demon from her. The Exorcist was a surprise hit, going from a small release to becoming one of the highest grossing films of all time. Horror writer Stephen King called it a source of inspiration for his work.

THE
EXORCIST

Directed by WILLIAM FRIEDKIN

was directed by Michael Cimino in 1978. It starred Robert De Niro, Christopher Walken, John Savage, John Cazale, Meryl Streep and George Dzundza. The story follows three Russian American steelworkers during the Vietnam War. When it was released, critics gave it great praise for the performances, as well as the way the working class were portrayed. On a technical level, the film was influential for utilizing Dolby noise reduction. It took five months just to create the soundtrack for the film.

ROBERT DE NIRO

A MICHAEL CIMINO FILM

THE DEER HUNTER

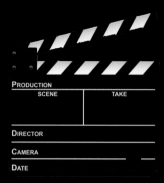

All Quiet on the Western Front

All Quiet on the Western Front was first a novel by Erich Maria Remarque, written in 1929. The movie was directed by Lewis Milestone and starred Lew Ayres and Louis Wolheim. The movie is about a group of young boys, including the main character, Paul Baumer, becoming inspired to join the army after hearing an impassioned speech from their professor. All Quiet on the Western Front was hailed for its realism in showing the horrors soldiers faced in World War I. It was one of the earlier movies to be placed in preservation by the National Film Registry.

that was produced in 1967. It was directed by Arthur Penn and starred Warren Beatty and Faye Dunaway as the titular characters. The story follows a romanticized account of the famous bank robbing couple and their gang. Bonnie and Clyde was a surprise hit. It was revolutionary at the time for breaking so many cinematic taboos, and making a younger audience interested in films. The film was famous for the way it displayed both sex and violence, with the climatic ending hailed as being one of the bloodiest death scenes ever shown on film.

The French Connection

The French Connection is a crime thriller, based on the non-fiction book of the same name by Robin Moore. It was directed in 1971 by William Friedkin and starred Gene Hackman, Fernando Rey, and Roy Scheider. The story is based on fictionalized versions of real life comes Eddie Egan and Sonny Grosso, who worked undercover to try and stop the largest heroin smuggling syndicate. The film was praised for the great cast, but also for having one of the most famous car chase scenes in cinematic history. As of 2015, it's still considered one of the best action movies to date.

GENE HACKMAN

FRENCH CONNECTION

City Lights

City Lights is a 1931 silent film that was produced, directed, written, and starred Charlie Chaplin. On top of all that, he also composed the music to the film. Virginia Cherrill, Florence Lee, and Harry Myers starred alongside Chaplin. The movie is about Chaplin's famous character, the Tramp, falling in love with a blind flower girl. It's considered to be Chaplin's finest movie, which is made all the more impressive by how involved Chaplin was on the production side as well as the acting side. Despite the era of silent films being over, it was still a huge cinematic hit.

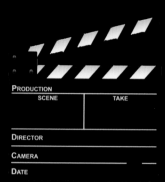

It Happened One Night

It Happened One Night was a comedy, directed by Frank Capra in 1934. It starred Claudette Colbert and Clark Gable. The story was loosely based on a short story, Night Bus, by Samuel Hopkins Adams. The story follows young socialite, Ellen Andrews, who wants to escape from her father. She ends up falling in love with a reporter, Peter Warne. It Happened One Night was the first movie to win all five of the major Academy Awards, a feat that, as of 2015, only 2 other movies have managed.

was partially based on Theodore Dreiser's novel, An American Tragedy. The movie starred Montgomery Clift, Elizabeth Taylor, and Shelly Winters. The story is about George Eastman, a poor bellhop who gets the chance to visit and work for his rich uncle. The movie did well for the time, although it hasn't necessarily aged well. Actor Charlie Chaplin famously called it the greatest movie about America that he had ever seen.

MONTGOMERY CLIFT

ELIZABETH TAYLOR

SHELLEY WINTERS

A GEORGE STEVENS PRODUCTION OF

A PLACE IN THE SUN

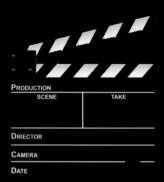

Midnight Cowboy

Midnight Cowboy is a drama, based on a book by James Leo Herlihy. It was directed in 1969 by John Schlesinger and starred Dustin Hoffman, Jon Voight, Sylvia Miles, and Brenda Vaccaro. The story is about Joe Buck, a young Texan who quits his job and runs off to New York to become a male prostitute. As of 2015, Midnight Cowboy is the only X rated film to have ever won an Oscar. Midnight Cowboy was praised for exploring darker themes and taking on subjects that were considered taboo in movies.

MGM DVD

A JEROME HELLMAN · JOHN SCHLESINGER Production

DUSTIN HOFFMAN   JON VOIGHT
MIDNIGHT COWBOY

BEST
PICTURE
1969

political comedy directed and produced by Frank Capra. It starred James Stewart and Jean Arthur. The movie follows the life of Jefferson Smith, who is selected to become a US Senator by corrupt politicians who hope to manipulate his naïveté and complete lack of political experience. At first the movie was hailed as being anti-American because it displayed corruption and scandal in American politics. Ultimately, it was this controversy that led to it being such a hit with audiences. It was also credited with launching James Stewart's acting career.

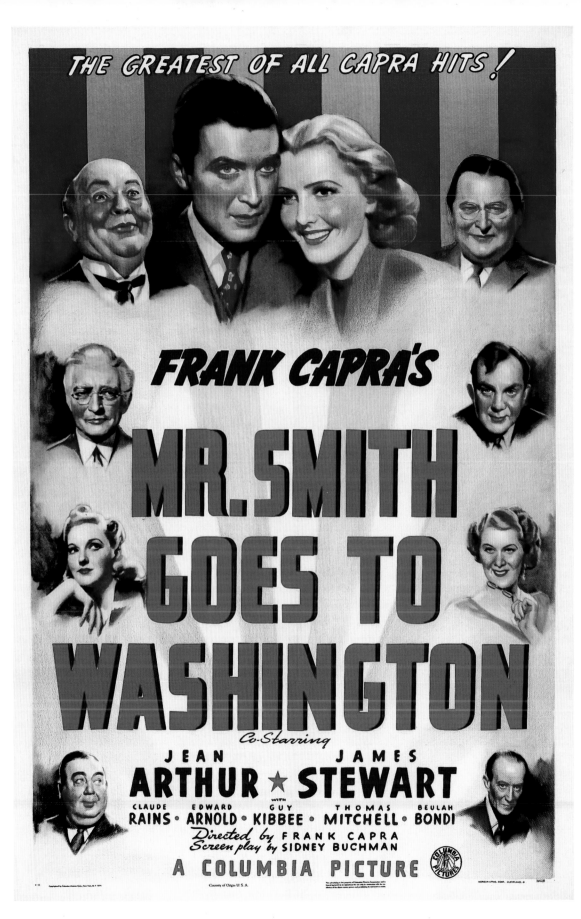

Rain Man

Rain Man is a 1988 drama, directed by Barry Levinson. It starred Dustin Hoffman, Tom Cruise, and Valeria Golino. The story is about Charlie Babbitt, a selfish car salesmen, who finds out that his father left everything to Charlie's autistic brother, Raymond. Charlie meets up with Raymond and the two decide to go on a road trip together. Hoffman was praised for his performance as Charlie, and he was credited with dispelling many misconceptions about autism. His performance felt very genuine, and audiences appreciated how respectful Hoffman was in his performance.

DUSTIN
HOFFMAN

TOM
CRUISE

RAIN MAN

Annie Hall

Annie Hall is a 1977 romantic comedy, directed and co-written by Woody Allen. It also starred Allen, along with Diane Keaton. The story follows a comedian, Alvy Singer, as he tries to figure out why his relationship with the titular Annie Hall fell apart. Annie Hall was considered revolutionary at the time, and it changed the way that comedies were viewed. Annie Hall was described as a comedy that was able to be serious and less focused on hijinks. Diane Keaton earned attention for her style in the movie, which had a direct impact on the fashion of the 70's.

PRODUCTION
SCENE   TAKE

DIRECTOR

CAMERA

DATE

Tootsie

Tootsie is a 1982 comedy, directed by Sydney Pollack. It starred Dustin Hoffman, Jessica Lange, Teri Garr, Dabney Coleman, and Charles Durning. The story follows Michael Dorsey, a respected actor that nobody is hiring because he's too difficult to work with. He decides to dress up as a woman out of desperation, hoping to get a role on a soap opera. The movie was being hailed as a return to the old style of whacky, absurdist comedies that started to become a relic of the past.

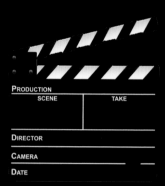

Fargo

Fargo is a comedy/crime thriller, written, produced, and directed by Joel and Ethan Coen in 1996. This dark film starred Frances McDormand, William H. Macy, Steve Buscemi, Harve Presnell, and Peter Stormare. The movie is about a pregnant police chief, Marge Gunderson, who has to solve a series of crimes being committed in her town. Fargo was a popular hit, with many film critics praising the way that the characters worked the setting into the story, helping to memorialize the characters.

FRANCES McDORMAND
FARGO

A LOT CAN
HAPPEN IN
THE MIDDLE
OF NOWHERE

Giant

Giant is a 1956 drama, directed by George Stevens. Stevens based the screenplay off of a 1952 novel by Edna Ferber. It starred Elizabeth Taylor, Rock Hudson, and James Dean. The story is about a Texas ranching family and everything that happened in their lives after World War II. Despite being critical of Texan society, it was still a huge hit in Texas. Stevens was praised for the way that he captured the beauty of Texas with his shots. It was the last movie that featured James Dean, who passed away before he could see it released.

The Grapes of Wrath

Grapes of Wrath was originally a 1939 novel, written by John Steinbeck. In 1940, it was turned into a film by director John Ford. It starred Henry Fonda, Jane Darwell, John Carradine, Shirley Mills, John Qualen and Eddie Quillan. The movie follows the story of the Joads, a family that lost their farm during the great depression and decide to move to California to look for work. It was one of the first 25 novels to be selected for preservation by the National Films Registry.

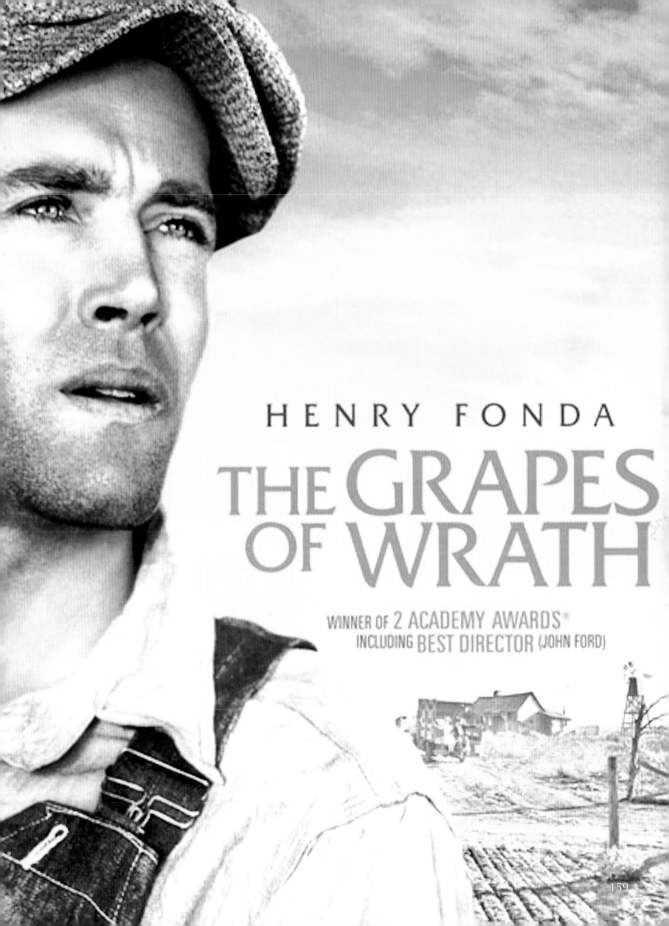

HENRY FONDA

THE GRAPES OF WRATH

WINNER OF 2 ACADEMY AWARDS*
INCLUDING BEST DIRECTOR (JOHN FORD)

Good Will Hunting

Good Will Hunting is a drama, directed by Gus Van Sant in 1997. It starred Matt Damon, Robin Williams, Ben Affleck, Minnie Driver, and Stellan Skarsgård. Affleck and Damon also co-wrote the film. The story follows Will Hunting, a 20 year old labourer who is an unrecognized genius. Good Will Hunting was praised for creating strong and original characters. Each actor brought those characters to life to create a box office hit. Good Will Hunting was shot for 10 million, and grossed just shy of 226 million worldwide.

GOOD WILL HUNTING

—— MOVIE SCREENING ——

Shane

Shane is a 1953 western film, directed by George Stevens, and based off a 1949 novel by Jack Schaefer. It starred Alan Ladd, Jean Arthur, Van Heflin, Brandon deWilde, and Jack Palance. It follows the story of the titular Shane, an iconic gunslinger that's looking to retire, but is pulled back into action against a ruthless cattle baron. Shane was an important movie since it was the first to be filmed in a widescreen format. It was also one of the first films to utilize hidden wires to perform stunts.

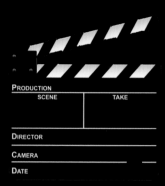

Terms of Endearment

Terms of Endearment was originally a novel by Larry McMurty. In 1983, James L. Brooks turned it into a film, which he directed, wrote, and produced. It starred Shirley MacLaine, Debra Winger, Jack Nicholson, Danny DeVito, Jeff Daniels, and John Lithgow. It follows the story of Aurora Greenway and Emma, her daughter, as they both try to find love. Critics praised it for its ability to tell a serious, heart wrenching story while still being a comedy. Jack Nicholson in particular was praised for his performance, even winning a Golden Globe for best supporting actor.

EBRA WINGER   SHIRLEY MacLAINE   JACK NICHOLSON

TERMS of ENDEARMENT

written by Stephen King. In 1999, Frank Darabont turned it into a crime drama, which he wrote, directed, and co-produced. It starred Tom Hanks, Michael Clarke Duncan, David Morse, Bonnie Hunt, and James Cromwell. The story follows John Coffey, an African American inmate assigned to death row for raping and killing two girls. The prison guards are surprised by how soft and gentle he is, as well as his ability to heal others. The Green Mile was over 3 hours long, something unheard of for most films, but it was still met with a great deal of critical praise.

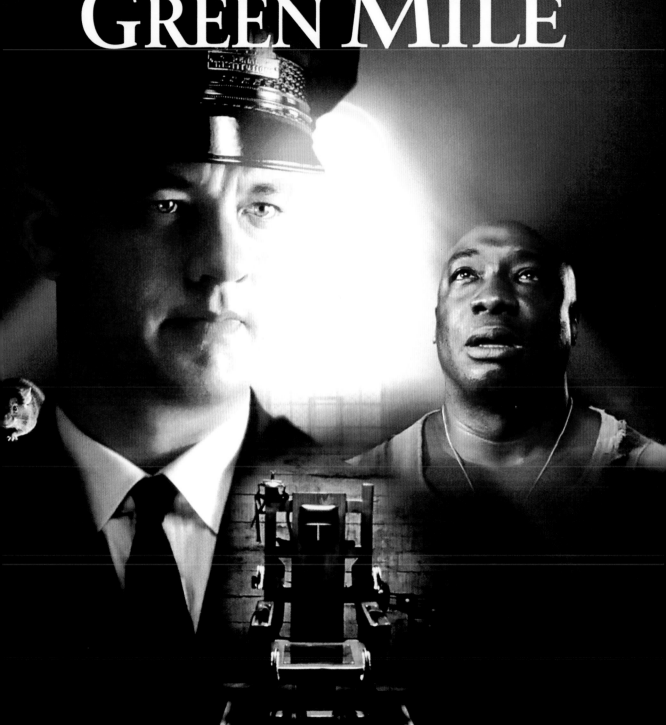

TOM HANKS

THE GREEN MILE

Close Encounters of the Third Kind

Close Encounters is a 1977 sci-fi film, written and directed by Steven Spielberg. It starred Richard Dreyfuss, Francois Truffaut, Melinda Dillon, Teri Garr, Bob Balaban, and Cary Guffey. The story follows an ordinary guy, Roy Neary, who encounters a UFO. Close Encounters had one of the highest budgets for visual effects, 3.3 million. The techniques used in Close Encounters went on to have a huge impact on motion control photography. It was also one of the first films to experiment with early CGI.

CLOSE ENCOUNTER
OF THE FIRST KIND
Sighting of a UFO

CLOSE ENCOUNTER
OF THE SECOND KIND
Physical Evidence

CLOSE ENCOUNTER
OF THE THIRD KIND
Contact

CLOSE ENCOUNTERS
OF THE THIRD KIND

Network

Network is a satirical film that was directed by Sidney Lumet, and written by Paddy Chayefsky. This 1976 film starred Faye Dunaway, William Holden, Peter Finch, and Robert Duvall. The movie follows a news anchor, Howard Beale, who discovers that his news program only has two weeks left on air because of poor ratings. In 2002, Network was given a place in the Producers Guild of America Hall of Fame for setting an enduring standard for American entertainment. Critics praised it for being an entertaining comedy, as well as delivering a strong message about how people view television and the news.

NETWORK

Still mad as hell after 30 years.

The Graduate

The Graduate was first a 1963 novel by Charles Webb. The movie was directed in 1967, by Mike Nichols. It starred Anne Bancroft, Dustin Hoffman, and Katharine Ross. It tells the tale of Benjamin Braddock, a recent college graduate, who doesn't know what to do with his life. He's seduced by Mrs. Robinson, but ultimately falls in love with her daughter, Elaine. It was a huge hit at the box offices. When adjusted for inflation, it ranks number 21 on the list of highest grossing films in the United States and Canada.

American Graffiti

American Graffiti is a movie, directed and co-written by George Lucas in 1973. It starred Richard Dreyfuss, Ron Howard, Paul Le Mat, Harrison Ford, Charles Martin Smith, Cindy Williams, Candy Clark, Mackenzie Philips, and Wolfman Jack. The movie follows a group of high school students on their final night before heading off to college. It was a low budget movie, filmed for under 1 million, and primarily was screened at festivals. Nevertheless, it went on to make over 200 million when it hit the box offices. Critics praised it for appealing to the nostalgia of the audience.

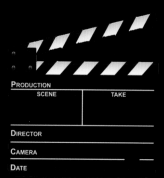

Pulp Fiction

Pulp Fiction was written and directed by Quentin Tarantino in 1994. It had a huge cast, including such famous actors as Samuel L. Jackson, Uma Thurman, Bruce Willis, Christopher Walken, and John Travolta. The story is told in a nonlinear fashion, following the lives of several different criminal characters. Tarantino was praised for his nonlinear storytelling, as well as his use of eccentric dialogue and managing to blend humour and violence together. Pulp Fiction is also credited with reviving John Travolta's acting career.

PULP FICTION

A FILM BY QUENTIN TARANTINO/PRODUCED BY LAWRENCE BENDER

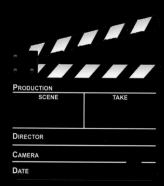

The African Queen

The African Queen was first a 1935 novel, written by C. S. Forester. The movie came out in 1951 and was directed by John Huston. It starred Humphrey Bogart, Katharine Hepburn, and Robert Morley. The story follows Samuel Sayer and his sister, Rose Sayer, acting as missionaries in an East African village at the start of World War I. The African Queen was one of the first movies to utilize Technicolor. It was also the only time that Humphrey Bogart won an Academy Award for his acting.

Mutiny on the Bounty

Mutiny on the Bounty is a 1935 drama, directed by Frank Lloyd. It was based on the novel of the same name by Charles Nordhoff and James Norman Hall. It starred Charles Laughton and Clark Gable. The story follows Fletcher Christian and his revolt against Captain Blight on the HMS Bounty. It was hailed as being one of the most important films of all time. There were many different adaptions of the Mutiny on the Bounty, but the 1935 film is considered to be the best adaptation of them all.

The Maltese Falcon

The Maltese Falcon is a 1941 film directed by John Huston, the very first film that he ever directed. It was based on a novel written by Dashiell Hammett. It starred Humphrey Bogart, Sam Spade, and Mary Astor. The movie follows two private investigators who take on a case involving a priceless statuette. At the time, it was considered one of the greatest thriller films ever made, and it was one of the first films preserved by the National Film Registry.